The Cold War

Wendy Conklin, M.A.

Publishing Credits

Historical Consultant
Shannon C. McCutchen

Editor
Torrey Maloof

Editorial Director
Emily R. Smith, M.A.Ed.

Editor-in-Chief
Sharon Coan, M.S.Ed.

Creative Director
Lee Aucoin

Illustration Manager
Timothy J. Bradley

Publisher
Rachelle Cracchiolo, M.S.Ed.

Teacher Created Materials
5301 Oceanus Drive
Huntington Beach, CA 92649-1030
http://www.tcmpub.com
ISBN 978-0-7439-0672-2

Table of Contents

What Is a Cold War?

During the 1900s, countries around the world fought an unusual war. This war lasted for more than 40 long years. It was unusual for a couple key reasons. First of all, this war had an unusual name. The world called it the Cold War. Second, it was not like any war the world had seen before. It was a battle between the East and the West, but they fired no shots. Instead, they fought with spies, space trips, sports, threats, the press, and by storing up weapons. Both sides tried to show off so they could say they were stronger than the other.

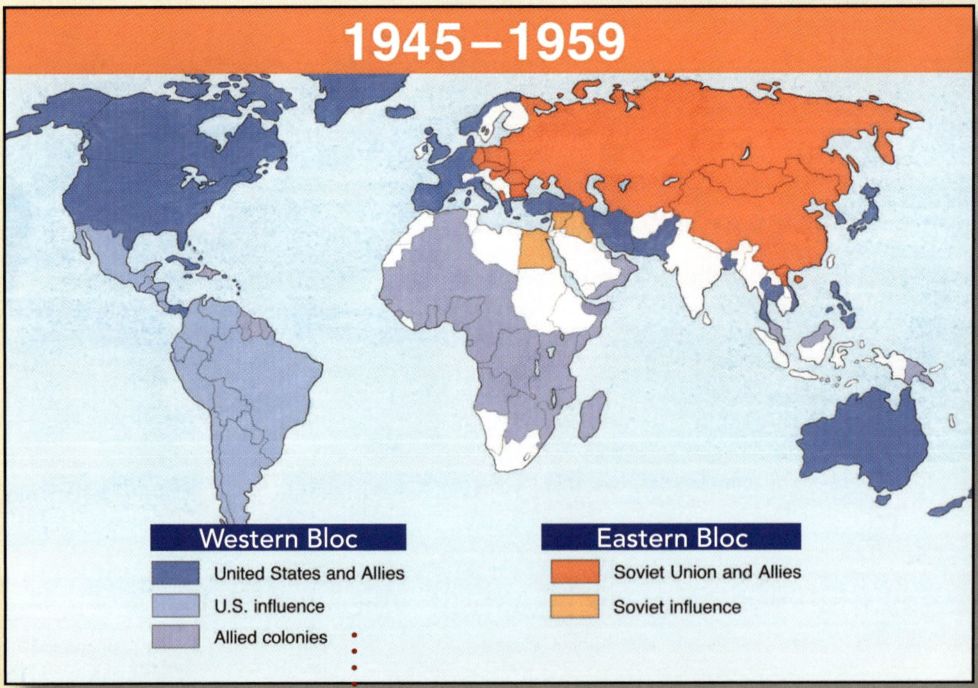

This map shows how the world looked from the end of World War II to 1959.

This rocket launcher is mounted on an armored truck.

Have you ever wondered what a cold war was? A *cold* war is the opposite of a *hot* war. Hot wars are full-blown wars with battles and full militaries involved. Both world wars are considered hot wars. A cold war is a war without battles. Cold wars are fought with words and threats. This is what happened in the world not too long ago.

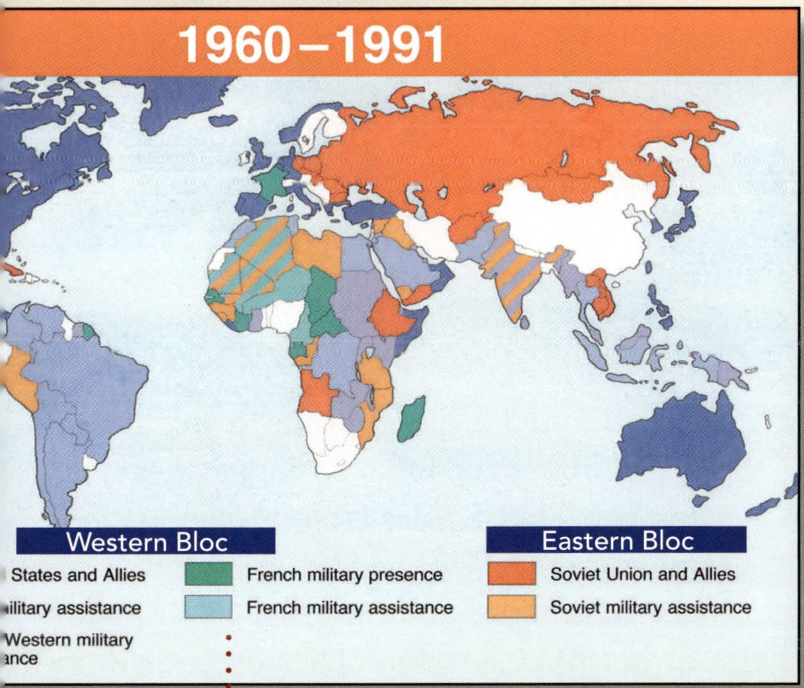

The world changed quite a bit during the last 30 years of the Cold War.

The Arms Race

The **arms race** was not about arms on a body. This type of *arms* means the same thing as *weapons*. During the Cold War, the world watched in fear as both sides made more and more nuclear (NOO-klee-uhr) weapons.

Friends Before, Friends No More

The East and West had been friends during World War II. They fought against the Nazis and won together. After the war, they became enemies. The major countries in the West included the United States, Great Britain, Japan, Canada, and France. The East mainly referred to countries controlled or supported by the Soviet Union.

Very Different Ideas

It all began with two countries. The United States of America was one of them. The Union of the Soviet Socialist Republics was the other. This country is also known as the Soviet Union or the USSR. The world called both countries superpowers because they were strong countries.

The leaders of the two governments did not agree on how to run a country. The Soviet Union had a **totalitarian** (toh-tah-luh-TAIR-ee-uhn) government. This meant that the leaders were in complete control. People living there were not free to do what they wanted. The United States has a **democracy** (dih-MAH-kruh-see). A democracy puts the power into the hands of the people. The **citizens** control the government by electing the leaders. People can speak their minds and control their own lives.

The United States and the Soviet Union had different **economic** (eh-kuh-NAH-mik) ideas, too. The Soviet Union followed **communism** (KAHM-yuh-nih-zuhm). In a Communist economy, the government controls all businesses. The government also

Karl Marx

Communism's Beginnings

Karl Marx was the father of communism. He believed everyone should have the same amount of money and land. He thought everyone would work hard for the government in return.

Opposites Do Not Attract

Communism and capitalism are opposite ideas. So are totalitarian and democratic governments. It would be hard to imagine that these opposites could live together in harmony.

owns all the land. All land and jobs are shared equally. No one has more than anyone else. The United States follows **capitalism** (KAP-uh-tuhl-iz-uhm). Capitalism allows people to own businesses. Instead of working for the government, people can work for themselves. In a capitalist country, there is often a wide gap between the rich people and the poor people.

Leaders in both of these countries thought their ideas on government and economics were right. They were afraid the other country wanted to destroy their way of life. As a result, these superpowers did not trust each other.

The red star soon came to symbolize communism. In the Soviet Union, it could be seen on buildings, planes, and military uniforms.

Curtains, Doctrines, and Plans

During World War II, the German Nazis had invaded the Soviet Union. Joseph Stalin was the Soviet leader. He did not want his country to be invaded ever again. So, he set up Communist leaders in the small countries around his borders.

Joseph Stalin led the Communist Soviet Union.

At that time, Winston Churchill was the leader of Great Britain. Stalin's actions in Eastern Europe worried him. In 1946, Churchill spoke about communism at a small college. He said an "iron curtain" had divided the East from the West. He meant that Stalin was forcing other countries to be like the Soviet Union. Many historians say the Cold War began the day Churchill gave this iron curtain speech.

After World War II, Europe was a mess. Factories were ruined, and there was not enough food to eat. So, the United States set up a program to help rebuild Europe. They called it the Marshall Plan. As part of the Marshall Plan, the United States sent money to Europe. All countries who wanted help received aid. Stalin felt this aid would spread capitalism. So, the Soviet Union and other Communist countries did not take part in this plan.

The many small countries in Eastern Europe were no match for the Soviet Union. Still, they tried to fight the growth of communism. To win this battle against communism, they needed money. Two countries that fought the USSR were Greece and Turkey. President Harry S. Truman created the Truman Doctrine. This plan provided money for Greece and Turkey. That way, they could buy weapons and supplies.

Winston Churchill led Great Britain at the beginning of the Cold War.

Taking Sides

The United States found allies in Western Europe to join them as they fought communism. This group of allies was called the North Atlantic Treaty Organization, or NATO. The Soviet Union's allies included countries in Eastern Europe. They were the Warsaw Pact.

Communism and Free Speech

Communist governments controlled their media. Churchill's iron curtain speech was not heard or published in the Soviet Union until 1998. This explains why people said the Soviets were behind an "iron curtain."

The Berlin Wall

Germany was in bad shape after World War II. To help rebuild the country, Germany was divided into sections. The Soviets controlled East Germany. France, Great Britain, and the United States controlled West Germany.

Germany's capital, Berlin, lay in the Soviet section of the country. Berlin was divided as well. The Soviets took charge of East Berlin. France, Great Britain, and the United States controlled West Berlin. West Berlin was an island in the middle of Soviet-controlled Germany.

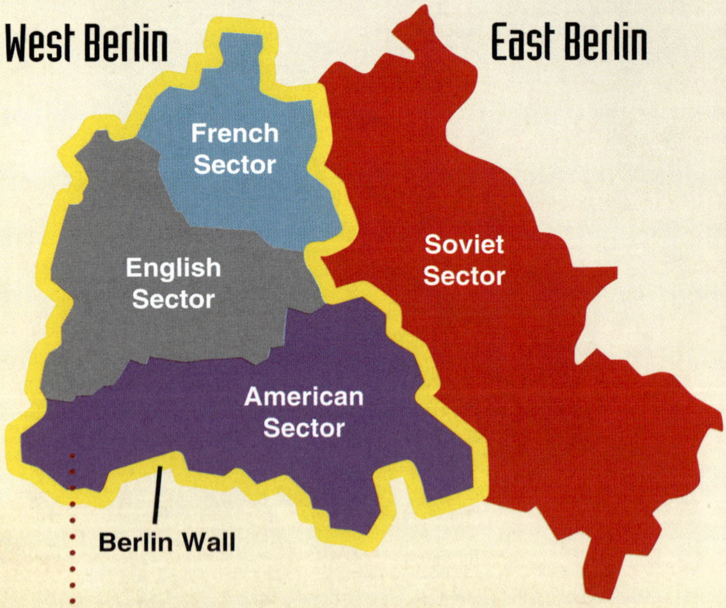

This graphic shows how the Berlin Wall was built around West Berlin. It kept the East Berliners from escaping into the sectors controlled by the West.

Building the Wall

The Berlin Wall was begun at midnight on August 13, 1961. Troops of the East German army first built fences to separate the city. Later, massive walls and trenches were built to keep people from fleeing to the West.

The Berlin Airlift

Pilots dropping food into West Berlin during that year saw many children. They took candy from their own food rations and dropped it for the children to enjoy.

By 1948, the Soviets and Americans could not agree on how to merge Berlin. The Soviets blocked the road that led into West Berlin for one whole year. The West had to **airlift** supplies into their part of the city.

Some people living in East Berlin escaped Soviet rule. They slipped across the dividing line into West Berlin. There they had more freedom. The Soviets felt they had to stop their people from leaving.

So, in 1961, the Soviets built a wall around West Berlin. The world called it the Berlin Wall. For more than 25 years, that wall stood as a visible reminder that the world was fighting the Cold War.

In November 1989, it was announced that people living in East Berlin could travel to West Berlin. People tore down the Berlin Wall with their bare hands, ropes, and sledgehammers.

A man uses a sledgehammer to help break down the Berlin Wall in 1989.

The Korean War

Korea (kuh-REE-uh) was divided into two parts at the end of World War II. It was separated at the **38th parallel**. The original plan was to rejoin the nation and let the citizens vote for new leaders. This never happened. The United States supported the South. They wanted to set up a capitalist country. The Soviet Union backed the North and its Communist leader. Eventually, fighting broke out at the 38th parallel. The South Koreans started the fighting. Then, on June 25, 1950, North Korea invaded South Korea.

The North had plenty of tanks and guns from the Soviet Union. China secretly decided to help them fight the war, too. Chinese leaders wanted to protect their own Communist government. The North began to win. Then, they captured the capital city of South Korea, Seoul (SOHL).

At that point, the United States rushed in to help the South. General Douglas MacArthur led the troops. He pushed the North back across the 38th parallel. The North pushed south and recaptured the capital. The fighting went back and forth for a while with no clear winner. The United States worried that this could turn into a third world war. On July 27, 1953, an **armistice** (ARE-muhs-tuhs) was signed. This document stopped the fighting. This was the first time the United States did not win a war it was fighting.

Mao Tse-tung and China helped North Korea during the Korean War.

General Douglas MacArthur (far right) and other officers at the front line in Korea.

The Korean peninsula

Fighting Through Others

There was never a military war directly between the Soviet Union and the United States during the Cold War. Instead, they fought each other indirectly. Each country helped a different side in Korea, Vietnam (vee-uht-NAM), and Afghanistan (af-GAN-uh-stan).

No Signature from the South

South Korea refused to sign the peace armistice. It was signed by the United States, the United Nations, North Korea, and China.

Communist China

In 1949, Mao Tse-tung (MAU-zuh-DUNG) was the new Communist leader of the People's Republic of China. He ruled for 27 years. He thought that if his people just worked hard enough, they could overtake the West.

Communism and the Great Depression

The Rosenbergs had been Communists when they were young. During the Great Depression, many people joined the Communist Party. Capitalism was not working, and people were looking for something that would help them. At that time, being a Communist was not a bad thing.

Two Sons

Ethel and Julius had two sons, Michael and Robert. During this time, Michael wrote a letter to President Dwight D. Eisenhower asking him to let his parents out of prison. They also carried protest signs in Washington, D.C., saying, "Don't Kill My Mommy and Daddy."

Executed

Ethel Rosenberg was the first woman executed in the United States since 1865.

Secrets and Spies

The Cold War was a time of many secrets. One big secret was how to make an **atomic bomb**. Scientists in the United States worked on making these bombs during the 1930s and 1940s. Quickly after that, the Soviet Union had an atomic bomb, too. The United States leaders believed that someone had shared important scientific secrets. The Federal Bureau of Investigation (FBI) decided to find these spies.

The United States dropped two atomic bombs on Japan during World War II.

The investigation led the FBI to a man and woman. Their names were Julius and Ethel Rosenberg. Ethel's brother, David Greenglass, told the FBI that she and Julius were spies. He claimed that Julius tried to get others to spy for the Soviet Union, also. Greenglass also said that Ethel typed up notes from secret meetings. In no time, Julius was arrested and held in prison. The court charged him with **espionage** (ES-pee-uh-nawj).

Julius did not want to talk to the FBI. This frustrated the government. He was put on trial. Ethel faced a trial, too. Both Julius and Ethel claimed to be innocent. Their case went all the way to the Supreme Court. In the end, they were found guilty of **conspiracy** to commit espionage. They both died in the electric chair on June 19, 1953.

EXTRA

RACE RESULTS — Los Angeles Times — PICTORIAL

EQUAL RIGHTS — LIBERTY UNDER THE LAW — TRUE INDUSTRIAL FREEDOM

VOL. LXXII — IN THREE PARTS ★★★ — SATURDAY MORNING, JUNE 20, 1953 — 42 PAGES — DAILY, 10¢

ROSENBERGS DIE

Pair Executed for Atom Spying

END OF TRAIL—Summons to death in electric chair come swiftly for Atom Spies Ethel and Julius Rosenberg after stay was revoked and clemency was refused.

Supreme Court and Eisenhower Reject Couple's Last Pleas

OSSINING, N.Y., June 19—Atom Spies Julius and Ethel Rosenberg died in Sing Sing Prison's electric chair shortly before sundown today. The executions followed quickly after the Supreme Court set aside a stay of execution granted Wednesday by Justice William O. Douglas and President Eisenhower's refusal to grant them clemency.

SING SING PRISON, N.Y., June 19 (UP) Atom Spies Julius and Ethel Rosenberg were ordered electrocuted late today for betraying their country's secrets to Russia and threatening the lives of millions by bringing the world closer to an atomic war.

The Justice Department set the time for the doomed couple's death in Sing Sing Prison's electric chair after a day of suspense in which the U.S. Supreme Court denied their final appeals and President Eisenhower again refused executive clemency.

Warden Wilfred Denno announced first the husband and wife espionage team would be put to death in the gray-walled prison's death chamber "before sundown," which comes at 8:30 p.m. (5:30 PDT) today at Sing Sing.

Later he said the first execution would come at 8 p.m. EDT with the second a few minutes later.

Newspapers across the country reported the execution of the Rosenbergs.

Witch Hunts and Fear

Many Americans feared that communism would take over the United States. By early 1950, the search was on for Communist spies. Senator Joseph McCarthy said that he had the names of spies in the U.S. government. During a speech, he waved this list and scared many people. McCarthy was not able to prove any of these **accusations** (ak-yoo-ZAY-shuhnz). Even so, his words ruined many lives. People lost their jobs, families, and friends just because he said they were Communists.

The House of Representatives formed a group of people to search for Communists in the United States. This group was the House Un-American Activities Committee (HUAC). The group targeted people in Hollywood. Many famous people were called

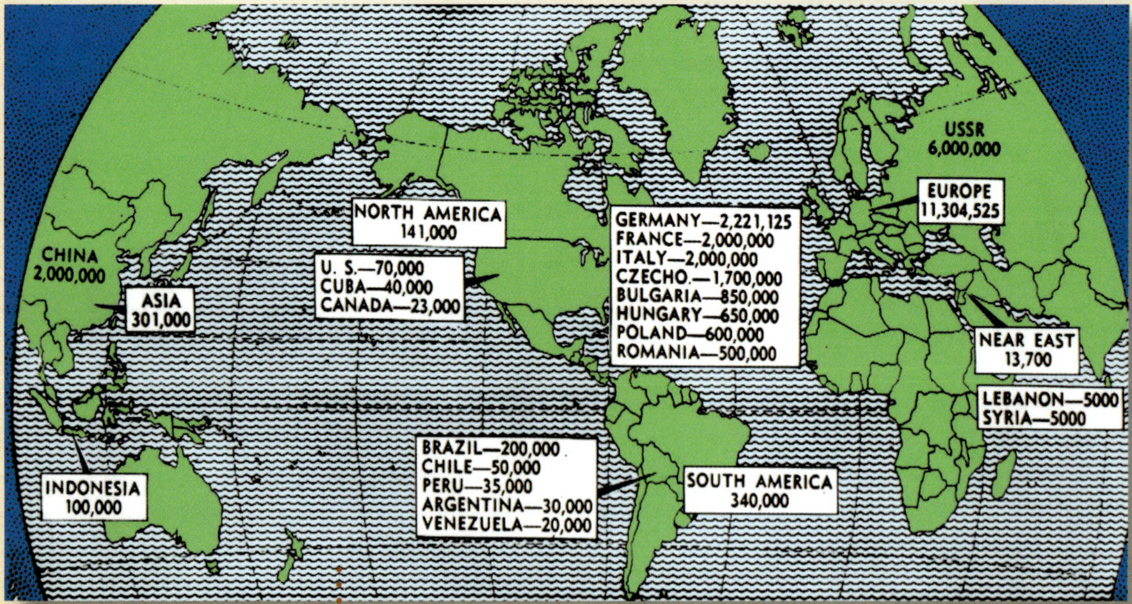

This map shows the numbers of Communist Party members around the world in 1947.

Senator McCarthy speaks about trying to find Communists in America.

before this committee. They were asked, "Are you now, or have you ever been, a member of the Communist Party?" If they did not answer, they were put in jail. Actors, directors, and writers could not find jobs anywhere. They were **blacklisted**!

Before this, Americans believed the Bill of Rights would protect them. It was as if being a Communist was against the law. All of a sudden, people found that they were not free to choose what they believed.

I'm No Communist!

Humphrey Bogart was a famous actor in the 1940s and '50s. He flew to Washington, D.C., to support his friends before HUAC. This backfired and people wondered if he was a Communist. He soon found that he had to campaign to clear his name.

An Angry Letter

President Harry S. Truman was angered by McCarthy. Truman wrote a letter to McCarthy that told him he should be ashamed of himself. However, some historians do not believe Truman ever sent the letter.

Nuclear Bombs

There were two types of nuclear bombs created in the 1940s and 1950s. The atomic bomb came before the hydrogen bomb. The atomic bomb explodes when big atoms split quickly. This releases energy. Hydrogen bombs get their amazing energy from little atoms joining together. Hydrogen bombs are 1,000 times more powerful than atomic bombs.

Radiating Comics

Marvel Comics decided to relate their superheroes to the times. Their comic books showed heroes affected by radioactivity. *The Incredible Hulk* told a story about a scientist affected by radioactivity. Nuclear fallout tainted *Spider-Man*, too. Peter Parker was bitten by a radioactive spider. And suddenly, he had amazing powers.

Nuclear Alarm

The creation of the atomic bomb spread fear around the world. The bombs dropped on Japan at the end of World War II showed their power. Then, the United States tested the first **hydrogen bomb** in 1952. By 1953, the Soviets had also created hydrogen bombs. Hydrogen bombs are much more powerful and scary than atomic bombs.

Scientists tested this hydrogen bomb by exploding it on January 14, 1954.

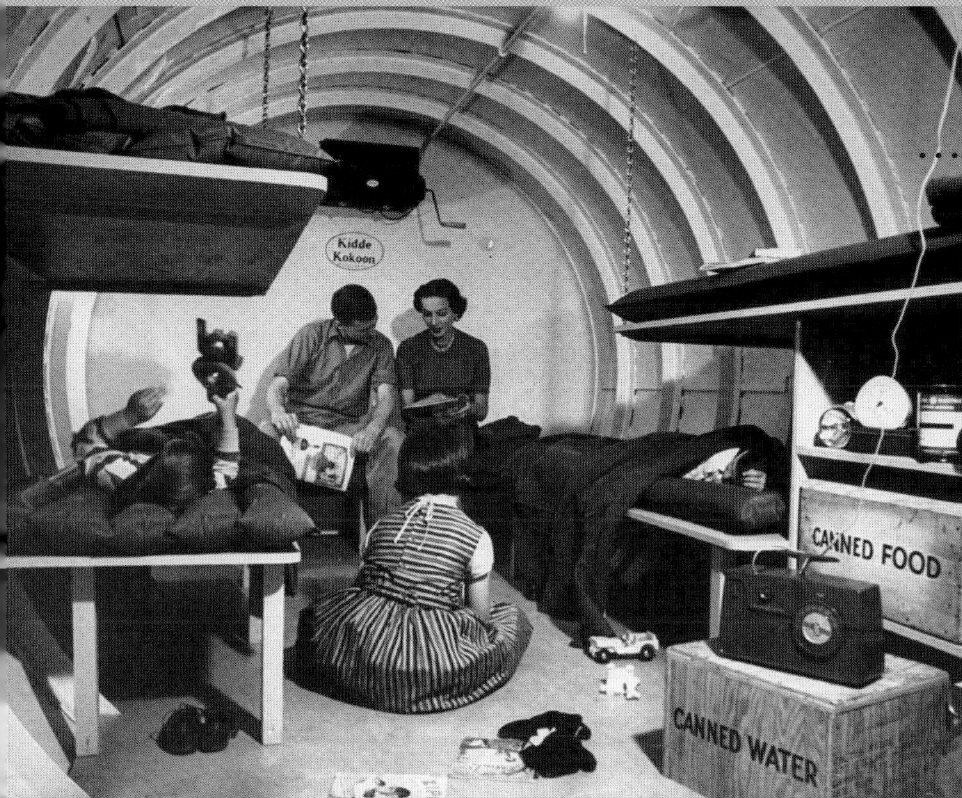

Some families built bomb shelters in their backyards. Bomb shelters contained canned food and water among other things.

Radioactivity became a concern in the United States. Scientists found it in baby's teeth and realized that it was in the food they ate. People quickly tried to learn more about this.

Nuclear fallout is what is left in an area after a nuclear explosion. The dust and air are very radioactive. Scientists tried to figure out how to protect everyone. First, children were taught to duck under their desks and cover their heads. It did not take long to realize this would not protect children during a nuclear attack.

Next, leaders developed **evacuation** plans. New highways were built to quickly move military troops. People also built their own **fallout shelters** stocked with food and supplies. They hoped they could survive in the shelters for weeks. The fear of nuclear attack was the hardest part of the Cold War for most people.

Racing to Space

The Germans were the first to build rockets during World War II. These rockets could send bombs 185 miles (300 km) away. After the war, scientists used these designs to build rockets for outer space. The Soviets built a rocket more quickly than the United States. On October 4, 1957, a Soviet **satellite** (SAT-uhl-lite) blasted into space. They called it *Sputnik I*. A month later, the Soviets sent a dog into space. This was the first living being sent into space. The United States tried to launch a satellite, but it failed.

Leaders in the United States knew they were behind in the space race. So, they created the National Aeronautics and Space Administration (NASA). On May 25, 1961, President John F. Kennedy said, "I believe that this nation should commit itself to achieving the goal, before this decade is out, of landing a man on the moon and returning him safely to the earth." NASA met this challenge head-on. On July 20, 1969, Neil Armstrong and Buzz Aldrin walked on the moon.

The space race was really about new technologies. Both countries developed intercontinental ballistic missiles (in-tuhr-kawn-tuh-NEN-tuhl buh-LIS-tik MIS-suhlz), or ICBMs. These missiles could carry nuclear bombs to other countries. This was the way governments showed their strength to each other and to the world.

When Neil Armstrong first stepped on the moon's surface, he said these famous words, "That's one small step for [a] man; one giant leap for mankind." This photograph shows Buzz Aldrin on the moon with the U.S. flag.

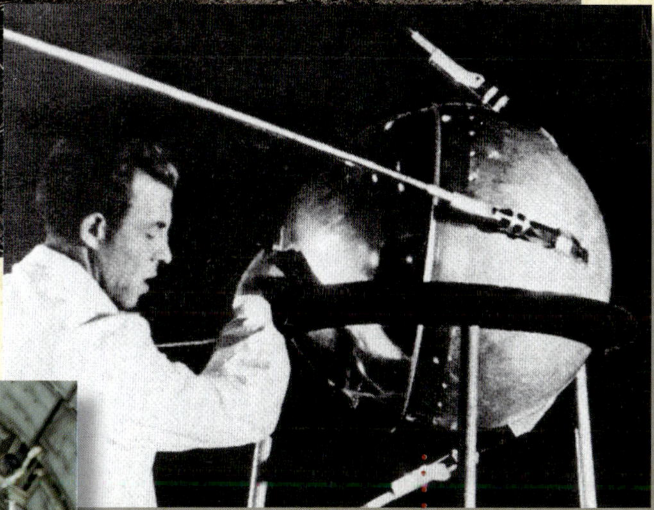

Sputnik I was successfully launched into space in 1957.

This is an intercontinental ballistic missile (ICBM).

Did You Know?

Technology was not only making space travel possible. It was also changing life on Earth. The first microwave oven was built in 1947. It weighed 750 pounds (340 kg). It was as tall as a man. Computers in the 1960s took up whole rooms. The Internet was first thought of in 1968. By the 1970s, it was used on a few college campuses. It did not become popular until the 1990s.

Space-Inspired Inventions

Freeze-dried foods were used to feed astronauts in space. Cordless tools were also first used by astronauts.

A Crisis in Cuba

In 1959, a man named Fidel Castro (fee-DEL KAS-troh) became the ruler of Cuba. He quickly made friends with leaders of the Soviet Union. The United States was worried. Cuba is only 90 miles (145 km) south of the United States.

The Central Intelligence Agency (CIA) had a secret plan. They found Cuban **exiles** (EK-zilez) willing to fight against Cuba. The CIA hoped these fighters could force Castro out of power. The troops secretly trained in Guatemala (gwah-tuh-MAH-luh).

Can You Keep a Secret?

The Cuban Missile Crisis ended because both sides agreed to disarm their missiles. The public was not told that Kennedy negotiated with Khrushchev. It was made to look like Kennedy won this disagreement without giving anything in return.

The Hot Line

The Cuban Missile Crisis made the leaders of each country realize how difficult it was to communicate during the crisis. At one point, a message was sent by bicycle messenger. So, a new way of communicating with each other was developed. It is called the Hot Line. A technologically advanced version still exists today.

Castro visited the United States in 1959. President Eisenhower refused to meet with him during the visit.

The U.S. Navy off the coast of Cuba during the Cuban Missile Crisis

In the meantime, President John F. Kennedy took office. The CIA told him of the plan. On April 15, 1961, the troops landed at the Bay of Pigs. This bay is on the southern coast of Cuba. But the attack fell apart. President Kennedy looked like a fool to leaders of the world when they found out that the United States was behind the plan.

The Soviet leader, Nikita Khrushchev (nih-KEY-tah KROOSH-chev), thought Kennedy was weak. So in October 1962, he set up nuclear missiles in Cuba. They were aimed at U.S. cities. Soviet ships carrying missiles sat in the waters off the United States. Kennedy set up a **naval blockade** of Cuba. He demanded that the Soviets take the missiles back to the Soviet Union. He also wanted all the missiles removed from Cuba. The Soviets wanted U.S. missiles removed from Turkey. After 13 days, both sides backed down. They narrowly avoided a nuclear war. This is called the Cuban Missile Crisis.

American helicopters drop soldiers off in a combat zone.

The Conflict in Vietnam

The terrible conflict in Vietnam started in the early 1950s. At that time, Vietnam was divided into two parts: North Vietnam and South Vietnam. The leader in the north was Ho Chi Minh (HOH-chee-MIN), and he was a Communist. The Soviets and Chinese assisted him with a fight against South Vietnam.

The United States decided to take a stand again. They sent money to help the South fight against the North Vietnamese Communists. The money was not enough. By the early 1960s, the United States sent troops to Vietnam. Soon, the United States was spending billions of dollars on this conflict.

In August 1964, two U.S. ships sat in Vietnam's Gulf of Tonkin (TAWN-kuhn). Reports that the ships had been attacked reached President Lyndon Johnson. Congress did not declare war, but it did pass the Gulf of Tonkin Resolution (rez-uh-LOO-shuhn). This resolution gave Johnson the power to use the military in Vietnam.

A war was never declared against North Vietnam. And yet, the conflict dragged on until 1975. At that time, the last U.S. troops were finally out of Vietnam.

French Rule in Asia

Before World War II, France ruled Indochina, which includes Vietnam, Laos (LAH-ows), and Cambodia. These countries were French colonies. The French were fighting in Vietnam for years before the United States arrived.

Drafting Soldiers

There were about 500,000 United States soldiers sent to Vietnam during the conflict. Some men had been in the military already. Others were **drafted** during the conflict.

Women in Vietnam

During the Vietnam era, women were not allowed to fight in combat. However, thousands of women wanted to serve the country. So, these women became nurses, Red Cross volunteers, photographers, therapists, assistants, and more.

Lyndon B. Johnson became president in 1963.

In Washington, D.C., a memorial reminds Americans that women served in this conflict.

Two Big Men

When President Ronald Reagan took office in 1981, things were not going well between the Soviet Union and the West. Reagan believed that the United States needed to build up its weapons. He could not let the Soviets believe his country was weak. At the same time, this buildup of arms frightened people. They worried about a nuclear war.

The Mark of a Leader

Gorbachev has a strange birthmark on his head. Some people thought this was a sign from the Bible that he would rule for seven years. They were close. He actually ended up ruling for six years.

Leading to Democracy

Before long, the changes Gorbachev made cost him his job. His country fell apart in 1991, and he resigned. Democracy had won, and the Soviet Union held free elections.

Mikhail Gorbachev and Ronald Reagan sign the treaty banning some nuclear missiles.

Researchers from the Strategic Defense Initiative stand next to a high-energy laser.

In response, the **Strategic Defense Initiative** (struh-TEE-jik duh-FENSE ih-NIH-shuh-tiv) began. Some people nicknamed this program "Star Wars." Could satellites in space destroy missiles in midair? Congress agreed to put money toward answering this question.

In the mid-1980s, Mikhail Gorbachev (mick-HAIL GORE-buh-chof) rose to power in the Soviet Union. He believed in communism, but he was a different kind of Communist. Gorbachev wanted to be on good terms with the West. He thought his country needed social and economic reform. He began to make changes.

Gorbachev and Reagan met to talk about reducing arms. They knew that nuclear weapons were not the answer. In December 1987, they signed a treaty. The Cold War was over by 1991.

The End of the Cold War

The Cold War ended because communism collapsed. This economic system did not work in the Soviet Union. People wanted to own land. They wanted the freedom to run their own businesses.

Although the Cold War did not always include battles, it was a real war. Both sides used spies to help them build better nuclear weapons. The arms race brought a new kind of fear to people. Coming close to nuclear war scared people all over the world.

The real fighting took place in smaller countries. The West learned hard lessons from the conflicts in Korea and Vietnam. One lesson was to fully understand the people in a country before going to war.

The East and West also battled by racing into outer space. The world changed as both sides tried to invent new technologies to stay ahead in the race.

The Cold War ended in the early 1990s. However, many of today's conflicts remind people of those hard years after World War II.

Both China and Cuba are still Communist countries today.

President George H. W. Bush and Mikhail Gorbachev

Richard Nixon was president of the United States from 1969–1974.

The Evil Empire

After his election, Ronald Reagan called the Soviet Union an evil empire. The West had gotten used to having an evil foe to fight. When the Cold War ended, it was hard to think of the new Russia as a friend.

Words for Gorbachev

Former U.S. President Nixon said of Gorbachev: "He has decided that he would risk his power in order to save his reforms, rather than risk his reforms in order to save his power." This means that Gorbachev truly believed in what he was fighting for in the Soviet Union.

Glossary

38th parallel—the dividing line between North and South Korea

accusations—charges of wrongdoing or crimes

airlift—a system of moving people or cargo by aircraft, usually to or from an area that cannot be reached otherwise

armistice—peace agreement; truce

arms race—a time when countries each try to produce the strongest weapons

atomic bomb—a nuclear bomb that releases energy by fission; used in World War II against the Japanese

blacklisted—to be added to a list of people who are not chosen for jobs

capitalism—an economic idea that lets people control their own businesses

citizens—people who have the right to live in a country because they were born there or people who have received the legal papers needed to live in a country

communism—an economic policy where the government distributes all land and goods equally to the people

conspiracy—when people work together in secret

democracy—a government system where the people elect the leaders

drafted—forced to join the military

economic—having to do with industry, trade, and finance

espionage—spying

evacuation—the removal of troops or people from a dangerous place

exiles—people who are sent away or deported from their homelands

fallout shelters—small, underground housing where people gathered in case of a nuclear attack

hydrogen bomb—a bomb whose power is due to the release of energy made when atoms unite

naval blockade—to block ships with other ships at sea

nuclear fallout—what is in the air and environment after a nuclear bomb explodes

radioactivity—when the center of an atom is unstable, it releases dangerous rays and particles

satellite—an object in space that orbits a larger object; a human-made object put into space to orbit Earth

Strategic Defense Initiative—an idea that satellites could destroy nuclear missiles before they reach their targets; nicknamed Star Wars

totalitarian—a political idea where the leaders are in complete control of a country

Index

Image Credits

cover Reuters/Corbis; p.1 Reuters/Corbis; p.4 The Woods Publishing Group; pp.4–5 The Woods Publishing Group; p.5 Cristian Marin/Shutterstock, Inc.; p.6 Photos.com; p.7 (left) Moyakov/Shutterstock, Inc.; p.7 (right) Darryl Sleath/Shutterstock, Inc.; p.8 Photos.com; p.9 Photos.com; p.10 (left) Betsy Morris; p.10 (right) Teacher Created Materials; p.11 Reuters/Corbis; p.12 The Library of Congress; pp.12–13 The Library of Congress; p.13 Government of the Republic of Korea; p.14 fotosav (Victor & Katya)/ Shutterstock, Inc.; p.14 Corbis; p.15 The Granger Collection, New York; p.16 The Library of Congress; p.17 (top) Bettmann/Corbis; p.18 (left) Yuriko Nakao/Reuters/Corbis; p.18 (right) The Library of Congress; p.19 Walter Sanders//Time Life Pictures/Getty Images; pp.20–21 (top) NASA; p.21 (middle) NASA; pp.20–21 (bottom) Steve Crise/Corbis; p.22 Library of Congress; p.23 The Granger Collection, New York; p.24 (top) The Granger Collection, New York; p24 (left) Ricardo.Martins/Flickr; p.24 (right) The Library of Congress; p.26 Bettmann/Corbis; p.27 Roger Ressmeyer/Corbis; p.28 (left) Dimitrios Kaisaris/Shutterstock; p.28 (right) erdem/Shutterstock, Inc.; p.29 (top) Mike Fisher/AFP/ Getty; p.29 (bottom) The Library of Congress